11+ Verbal Activity

CEM Style Cloze Activity Tests

TESTBOOK 7

Dr Stephen C Curran
with Warren Vokes

Edited by Katrina MacKay & Andrea Richardson

This book belongs to

ae TUITION

Accelerated Education Publications Ltd.

Guidance Notes for Parents

Cloze procedure involves supplying missing words or parts of words that have been deleted from a portion of text. Cloze tests require the ability to understand context and vocabulary in order to identify the correct words or parts of words that belong in the deleted passages of text.

Cloze passages include various forms of text:

- **Historical**
- **Biographical**
- **General Knowledge**
- **Literary Text - Prose**
- **Literary Text - Poetry**

There are three question types:

- **Missing Letters**
  In Missing Letters style questions the Cloze passage has a number of words where letters have to be provided to complete the word.

- **Multiple-choice**
  In Multiple-choice style questions there are three alternatives for the missing word in the Cloze passage.

- **Word Bank**
  In Word Bank style questions there are a number of alternatives provided in a set of words at the top of the page. Words are chosen from this Word Bank to fill the spaces in the Cloze passage.

Marking and Feedback

- The answers are provided at the back of this book.
- Only these answers are allowed.
- One mark should be given for each correct answer.
- Do not deduct marks for wrong answers.
- Do not allow half marks or 'the benefit of the doubt', as this might mask a child's need for extra help in the topic.
- Always try to be positive and encouraging.
- Talk through any mistakes with your child and work out together how to arrive at the right answer, using a dictionary if necessary.

Cloze Activity Test 1

Choose the correct words from the word bank below to complete the passage.

brink	**sailing**	**flowers**	**rose**	**mellow**
float	**twilight**	**barley**	**swan**	**clouds**

What is pink? a **1)** _______________ is pink
By the fountain's **2)** _______________ .
What is red? a poppy's red
In its **3)** _______________ bed.
What is blue? the sky is blue
Where the clouds **4)** _______________ through.
What is white? a **5)** _______________ is white
6) _______________ in the light.
What is yellow? pears are yellow,
Rich and ripe and **7)** _______________ .
What is green? the grass is green,
With small **8)** _______________ between.
What is violet? **9)** _______________ are violet
In the summer **10)** _______________ .
What is orange? why, an orange,
Just an orange!

What is pink? by Christina Rossetti (1830-1894).

Score [ ] **Percentage** [%]

Cloze Activity Test 2

Select the correct words to complete the passage below.

Born in Paddington in 1857, Robert Baden-Powell was the **1)** [ ] founder [ ] product [ ] ruler of the Scouting movement. He **2)** [ ] forfeited [ ] damaged [ ] pursued a career in the military and was the garrison commander at the Siege of Mafeking. Following the **3)** [ ] started [ ] lifting [ ] remains of the siege, he was **4)** [ ] promoted [ ] reduced [ ] demoted to Major-General and became a **5)** [ ] statutory [ ] revered [ ] fallen national hero. On his return from Africa in 1903, Baden-Powell **6)** [ ] learnt [ ] doubted [ ] thought that his military training **7)** [ ] schedule [ ] exercise [ ] manual , *Aids to Scouting*, had become a best-seller, and was being used by teachers and youth **8)** [ ] organisations [ ] employers [ ] councils . He decided to re-write *Aids to Scouting* to **9)** [ ] test [ ] relish [ ] suit a youth readership. In August 1907 he held a camp on Brownsea Island to test out his **10)** [ ] ideas [ ] tents [ ] recipes . The first book on the Scout Movement, Baden-Powell's *Scouting for Boys* was published in six

11) ☐ episode ☐ years ☐ instalments in 1908, and has sold **12)** ☐ approximately ☐ exactly ☐ under 150 million copies

as the fourth best-selling book of the 20th century. In January 1912, while

13) ☐ returning ☐ flying ☐ en route to New York on a Scouting World Tour, he met Olave St. Clair

Soames. They became **14)** ☐ friends ☐ rich ☐ engaged in September of the same year, causing a

media **15)** ☐ sensation ☐ blizzard ☐ flop due to Baden-Powell's fame, and married in private on 30

October 1912. The Scouts of England each **16)** ☐ charged ☐ donated ☐ received a penny to buy Baden-

Powell a wedding gift, a car. In 1920, the 1st World Scout **17)** ☐ Jamboree ☐ Circus ☐ Fair took

place in Olympia in West Kensington, and Baden-Powell was **18)** ☐ exonerated ☐ excused ☐ acclaimed

Chief Scout of the World, in 1929. Baden-Powell died in 1941. His gravestone

19) ☐ creates ☐ hides ☐ bears a circle with a dot in the centre "⊙", which is the **20)** ☐ road ☐ new ☐ trail sign

for "Going home", or "I have gone home".

Score ☐ **Percentage**

Cloze Activity Test 3

Choose the correct words from the word bank below to complete the passage.

bankrupt	**efficiency**	**aptitude**	**credited**	**employed**
ingenuity	**original**	**hauled**	**exploit**	**adaptation**

Richard Trevithick, born in Redruth in 1771, was a mining engineer who invented many **1)** _______________ machines. They include the screw propeller; the iron ship; a steam carriage; a steam-powered barge; and the first full scale steam-powered locomotive. James Watt is **2)** _______________ with the invention of the steam engine, but his was a low-pressure engine. Trevithick's design was driven by high-pressure steam, thereby increasing its power and **3)** _______________ . His first steam engine was used, from 1802, at an ironworks in Merthyr Tydfil, to drive a steam hammer, but his **4)** _______________ enabled him to see that the engine could be **5)** _______________ to power a transport system. In 1804, Trevithick adapted the basic single-cylinder engine with a flywheel arrangement by adding a draught-improving combined steam exhaust and chimney. This **6)** _______________ set the standard for all future steam locomotives. Using a metal track, the engine **7)** _______________ five wagons, containing ten tons of iron ore and 70 passengers, a distance of ten miles in a trip that took just over four hours to complete. Unfortunately, Trevithick's engineering talent was not matched by any commercial **8)** _______________ . He died in 1833, **9)** _______________ and in debt. However, he gained a place in history with his greatest achievement: he had laid the foundation for the first use of steam locomotives that others, like George Stevenson, would develop and **10)** _______________ .

Score ______ **Percentage** ______ %

Cloze Activity Test 4

Select the correct words to complete the passage below.

A GPO postal worker, named Patrick McKenna, and known by the **1)** ☐ nickname ☐ title ☐ question of *The Ulsterman*, had **2)** ☐ fortune ☐ surprise ☐ knowledge of the large amounts of bank notes being **3)** ☐ amassed ☐ printed ☐ carried by British Rail trains. He passed that information to Gordon Goody and Buster Reynolds, who planned the Great Train Robbery of 1963. Their **4)** ☐ boisterous ☐ criminal ☐ female gang had no **5)** ☐ competence ☐ trouble ☐ experience of stopping and robbing trains, so they **6)** ☐ entitled ☐ enacted ☐ enlisted the help of *The South Coast Raiders*, which included a specialist in **7)** ☐ rigging ☐ washing ☐ combing trackside signals. In the early hours of 7th August, the gang stopped and robbed the post office train **8)** ☐ travailing ☐ travelling ☐ trundling from Glasgow to Euston, which contained 72 post office staff that **9)** ☐ posted ☐ painted ☐ sorted the mail during the journey. They **10)** ☐ stole ☐ printed ☐ withdrew bank notes to the value of between £2.5 and £3 million pounds.

Score ☐ **Percentage** ☐ %

Cloze Activity Test 5

Fill in the missing letters to complete the passage below.

Construction of two **1)** p r _ t o t _ p e _ of the turbojet-powered supersonic passenger airliner began in February 1965: 001, built by Aerospatiale at Toulouse, and 002, by BAC at Filton, Bristol. It was named *Concorde* to reflect the Anglo-French **2)** t _ e _ t _ which led to its development and construction. The name *Concorde* is from the French word 'concorde', which has an English **3)** e q _ i v _ l _ n t , 'concord'. Both words mean agreement, harmony or union. At the time *Concorde* was developed, the world was a different place with hopes and **4)** _ s p i _ a t i o _ s that **5)** t e _ _ n o l _ g i _ a l advances would change the world we live in. On the afternoon of 2nd March 1969, *Concorde* 001 prepared to take off on its **6)** _ a i d e _ flight from the runway at Toulouse. The beautiful 'great white dart', flying at **7)** _ u _ e r s o _ i _ speed, would reduce the journey time from London to New York to three and a half hours instead of eight. It would bring continents and **8)** m _ n _ i n d closer together. *Concorde* 001 had been forced to wait on the ground for several days due to **9)** i _ c l e m _ n t weather. At the controls was the French test pilot, Andre Turcat, with co-pilot, Jacques Guignard, beside him in the cockpit. Also in the aircraft were two engineers, while the British test pilot, Brian Trubshaw, **10)** _ b s e r _ e _ from the ground. *Concorde* was loaded with about ten tons of **11)** i _ s t r u _ e n t a _ i o _ to record every aspect of the flight, and two chase aircraft would accompany the flight to independently verify the speeds and film the flight from close by. At 15.40hrs *Concorde* **12)** t h _ n d e _ e _ down the runway for almost a mile before lifting its long, drooping, dart-like nose, and taking off for the first time. The hoards of journalists and news crews burst into **13)** s _ o n t a n _ _ u s applause as the four Rolls Royce *Olympus* jet engines thrust the magnificent and graceful double delta-shaped winged aircraft into the sky. The flight, as planned, was kept simple; neither the droop nose, designed for better **14)** v i _ i _ i l _ t y when landing, nor the landing gear was raised during the 27 minute flight. Test pilot Trubshaw flew the aircraft **15)** _ a n _ a l _ y for the duration of the flight, taking *Concorde* to a speed of only 300mph. The first airborne journey passed **16)** u _ e v _ n t _ u l l _ , unlike the second, from British soil, when Brian Trubshaw had to land the aircraft with both altimeters **17)** i _ o p _ r a t _ v e . *Concorde* first flew supersonic, exceeding the speed of Mach 1, on its 45th flight in October 1969. *Concorde* was in service with four carriers: Air France, British Airways, Braniff International Airways and Singapore Airlines. It was finally **18)** w i _ h d _ a _ n in 2003. Although it was never a commercial success, *Concorde* proved to be a **19)** _ a g n i f i _ e n _ symbol of engineering **20)** g e n _ _ s .

Score [ ] **Percentage** [%]

Cloze Activity Test 6

Select the correct words to complete the passage below.

The discovery that there were oil **1)** ☐ mines ☐ tanks ☐ reserves under the North Sea justified British Petroleum's belief that their **2)** ☐ curiosity ☐ prospecting ☐ reports would reap rewards. Until the discovery, Britain **3)** ☐ relied ☐ stood ☐ existed wholly on importing OPEC's oil from countries in Africa, The Middle East and South America to satisfy the country's daily **4)** ☐ ration ☐ delivery ☐ consumption of two million barrels. On 3rd November 1975, the Queen pushed the red button to **5)** ☐ commence ☐ holt ☐ overcome the pumping ashore and production of North Sea Oil. The Forties oilfield **6)** ☐ wasted ☐ signed ☐ provided up to a quarter of Britain's oil consumption and taxation revenue **7)** ☐ swelled ☐ reduce ☐ broke the exchequer's **8)** ☐ building ☐ head ☐ coffers . It is estimated that around 76% of the North Sea oil reserves has already been **9)** ☐ spent ☐ extracted ☐ created so the oil bonanza may be coming to a **10)** ☐ conclusion ☐ record ☐ summit .

Score ☐ **Percentage** ☐ %

Cloze Activity Test 7

Choose the correct words from the word bank below to complete the passage.

baby	**worried**	**blunders**	**rode**	**crown**
churches	**cats**	**world**	**courted**	**buttercups**

If the butterfly **1)** ________________ the bee,
And the owl the porcupine;
If **2)** ________________ were built in the sea,
And three times one was nine;
If the pony **3)** ________________ his master,
If the **4)** ________________ ate the cows,
If the **5)** ________________ had the dire disaster
To be **6)** ________________ , sir, by the mouse;
If mamma, sir, sold the **7)** ________________
To a gypsy for half a **8)** ________________ ;
If a gentleman, sir, was a lady, —
The **9)** ________________ would be Upside-down!
If any or all of these wonders
Should ever come about,
I should not consider them **10)** ________________ ,
For I should be inside-out!

Topsy-Turvy World by William Brighty Rands (1823-1882).

Score [ ] **Percentage** [%]

Cloze Activity Test 8

Fill in the missing letters to complete the passage below.

There was, in fact, no part of his duty that the Reverend Mr. Mordaunt found so decidedly **1)** u _ p _ e a _ a n t as that part which compelled him to call upon his noble patron at the Castle. His noble patron, indeed, usually made these visits as **2)** _ i s a g _ e e a _ l e as it lay in his lordly power to make them. He **3)** a b h _ r r _ d churches and charities, and flew into violent rages when any of his tenantry took the **4)** l i _ e r t _ of being poor and ill and needing assistance. When his gout was at its worst, he did not **5)** h _ s i t _ t _ to announce that he would not be bored and **6)** _ r r i t _ t e _ by being told stories of their miserable misfortunes; when his gout troubled him less and he was in a somewhat more **7)** h u _ a n _ frame of mind, he would perhaps give the rector some money, after having bullied him in the most painful manner, and **8)** b _ r a t _ _ the whole parish for its shiftlessness and imbecility. But, whatsoever his mood, he never failed to make as many **9)** s a _ c a s _ i c and embarrassing speeches as possible, and to cause the Reverend Mr. Mordaunt to wish it were proper and Christian-like to throw something heavy at him. During all the years in which Mr. Mordaunt had been in charge of Dorincourt parish, the **10)** r _ c t _ r certainly did not remember having seen his lordship, of his own free will, do any one a kindness, or, under any **11)** c _ r c u _ s t _ n _ e s whatever, show that he thought of any one but himself. He had called to-day to speak to him of a specially **12)** p _ e s _ i n _ case, and as he had walked up the avenue, he had, for two reasons, **13)** d r e _ d e _ his visit more than usual. In the first place, he knew that his lordship had for several days been suffering with the gout, and had been in so **14)** v i _ l a _ n o _ s a humour that rumours of it had even reached the village—carried there by one of the young women servants, to her sister, who kept a little shop and **15)** r _ t _ i l e d darning-needles and cotton and peppermints and gossip, as a means of earning an **16)** _ o n e _ t living. What Mrs. Dibble did not know about the Castle and its inmates, and the farm-houses and their inmates, and the **17)** v i l l _ _ _ and its population, was really not worth being talked about. And of course she knew everything about the Castle, because her sister, Jane Shorts, was one of the upper housemaids, and was very friendly and **18)** i _ t i m _ t _ with Thomas.

"And the way his lordship do go on!" said Mrs. Dibble, over the counter, "and the way he do use **19)** l _ n g _ a g _ , Mr. Thomas told Jane herself, no flesh and blood as is in livery could stand—for throw a plate of toast at Mr. Thomas, hisself, he did, not more than two days since, and if it weren't for other things being **20)** _ g r _ e a _ l e and the society below stairs most genteel, warning would have been gave within a' hour!"

Extract from *Little Lord Fauntleroy*
by Frances Hodgson Burnett (1849-1924).

Score [ ] **Percentage**

Cloze Activity Test 9

Choose the correct words from the word bank below to complete the passage.

pursue	**complained**	**trial**	**patented**	**immunising**
popularly	**mauled**	**sour**	**growth**	**discoveries**

Louis Pasteur (1822-1895) was a French chemist and microbiologist who is renowned for his **1)** _______________ of the principles of microbial fermentation, pasteurisation and vaccination.

In 1856, he was approached by a local manufacturer of wine who **2)** _______________ that, when making beetroot alcohol, the wine would **3)** _______________ after a short while in storage. Pasteur's research into fermentation showed that the **4)** _______________ of micro-organisms was responsible for spoiling beverages, such as beer, wine and milk. By heating liquids to a temperature of between 60 and 100°C, he discovered that most bacteria were killed. He **5)** _______________ the process and the method became known as Pasteurisation.

This knowledge led him to **6)** _______________ the notion that micro-organisms caused infection in animals and humans. He began looking at the cause of chicken cholera and developed a vaccine which, by **7)** _______________ them against it, prevented infection. Vaccines against anthrax in cattle and rabies in dogs followed. The first human **8)** _______________ took place in 1885 on a nine year old boy who had been **9)** _______________ by a rabid dog. The boy showed no sign of infection and Pasteur was hailed as a hero.

He is **10)** _______________ known as the "father of microbiology".

Score ☐ **Percentage**

Cloze Activity Test 10

Select the correct words to complete the passage below.

To prevent the spread of infectious **1)** [☐ diseases ☐ noises ☐ spores], the chain of infection needs to be broken by a process known as hygiene. Most hygiene practices were **2)** [☐ rejected ☐ divulged ☐ developed] in the 19th century and were well **3)** [☐ established ☐ forgotten ☐ patented] by the mid-20th century. They are practised in the home, hospitals, food processing plants and animal **4)** [☐ happiness ☐ bones ☐ husbandry]. Simple routines, such as washing hands **5)** [☐ gingerly ☐ thoroughly ☐ quickly] before preparing or eating food, or between examining patients in hospital, are **6)** [☐ sufficient ☐ avoided ☐ unlikely] to prevent the spread of viruses. This simple precaution removes infectious **7)** [☐ odours ☐ fumes ☐ microbes] as well as dirt and grime. Keeping all work surfaces and kitchen **8)** [☐ utilities ☐ utensils ☐ utilises] clean to prevent cross-contamination, and **9)** [☐ sterilising ☐ cooling ☐ sharpening] surgical instruments in hospital theatres minimises the risk of infection from the spreading of **10)** [☐ germs ☐ gels ☐ saliva].

Score ☐ **Percentage** ☐ %

Cloze Activity Test 11

Fill in the missing letters to complete the passage below.

In the 20th century, demand for electricity led to the

1) c _ n s _ d e r _ t i _ n of geothermal power as a generating source. The world's oldest geothermal district heating system in Chaudes-Aigues, France, has been operating since the 14th century. The first geothermal power **2)** g _ n e _ a _ o r was tested by Prince Piero Ginori Conti in 1904, at the Larderello dry steam field where geothermal acid **3)** _ x t r a _ t i _ n began. The generator successfully lit four light bulbs. Later, in 1911, the world's first **4)** c o _ m e _ c i _ l geothermal power plant was built there. It was the world's only industrial producer of geothermal electricity until New Zealand built a **5)** _ l a n _ in 1958. The heat pump, used to draw heat from the ground, was **6)** i n _ e n t e _ by Lord Kelvin in 1852 and, in 1912, a patent for the idea was **7)** g _ a n t _ d to Heinrich Zoelly. However, it was not until the late 1940s that the geothermal heat pump was successfully **8)** i m p _ e m e _ t e _ . Geothermal energy is heat **9)** d r a _ _ from the earth, which is used as an affordable and **10)** s _ s t a _ n a _ l e solution to reducing dependence on fossil fuels. In the United States, more than 40 geothermal plants, which account for 80% of the nation's **11)** c a _ a c _ t y , are located in California and provide nearly 7% of the state’s electricity. Heat pumps

12) [u][ ][i][l][i][ ][e] the steady temperatures found just underground to provide heating and cooling for thousands of buildings across the United States. In Iceland, the world leader in direct applications, over 90% of its homes are

13) [ ][e][a][t][ ][d] with geothermal energy, saving Iceland over $100 million annually in avoided oil **14)** [i][ ][p][o][ ][t][s] . Reykjavík has the world's biggest district heating system and, while it was once the most

15) [p][ ][ ][l][u][t][ ][d] city in the world, it is now one of the cleanest. It confirms that geothermal energy is a source of clean and inexpensive power. To explain geothermal energy and how it is generated, it is necessary to look beneath the Earth’s surface. Below the **16)** [c][ ][u][s][ ] , there is a layer of hot and molten rock, called magma, in which **17)** [d][ ][c][a][y][ ][ ][g] natural radioactive materials, such as uranium and potassium, are a continual source of heat production. The difference in temperature between the core of the planet and its surface, known as the geothermal gradient, drives a continuous

18) [c][ ][n][d][ ][c][t][i][ ][n] of thermal energy in the form of heat from the core to the surface. At a depth of 10,000 metres below the surface of the Earth, the amount of heat contains 50,000 times more energy than all the oil and

19) [ ][a][t][u][r][ ][l] gas resources in the world. The areas where the highest underground temperatures may be found are in regions with

20) [a][ ][t][i][ ][e] or geologically young volcanoes.

Score [ ] **Percentage** [ ] **%**

Cloze Activity Test 12

Select the correct words to complete the passage below.

The elephant, thanks to the **1)** [☐ poor ☐ random ☐ skilful] guidance of the Parsee, was advancing rapidly through the still darksome forest, and, an hour after leaving the pagoda, had crossed a vast **2)** [☐ plain ☐ ocean ☐ hill]. They made a **3)** [☐ halt ☐ mistake ☐ rush] at seven o'clock, the young woman being still in a state of complete **4)** [☐ excitement ☐ prostration ☐ darkness]. The guide made her drink a little brandy and water, but the drowsiness which **5)** [☐ covered ☐ helped ☐ stupefied] her could not yet be shaken off. Sir Francis, who was familiar with the **6)** [☐ benefits ☐ justice ☐ effects] of the intoxication produced by the **7)** [☐ fumes ☐ clouds ☐ streams] of hemp, reassured his companions on her account. But he was more **8)** [☐ pleased ☐ disturbed ☐ stern] at the prospect of her future **9)** [☐ wealth ☐ features ☐ fate]. He told Phileas Fogg that, should Aouda remain in India, she would **10)** [☐ inevitably ☐ sometimes ☐ studiously] fall again into the hands of her executioners.

Extract from *Around the World in Eighty Days*
by Jules Verne (1828-1905).

Score [   ] **Percentage** [%]

Cloze Activity Test 13

Choose the correct words from the word bank below to complete the passage.

capability	**lethal**	**administered**	**fangs**	**sting**
predator	**inject**	**evolved**	**toxins**	**allergic**

Many animals use venom to kill their prey. They may bite, **1)** ________________ or use another part of their body to inject the deadly substance into their victim. The diet of venomous animals has also **2)** ________________ to include the venomous substance without harming the **3)** ________________ . The venom secreted by different animals is highly specialised and is specifically designed to deliver a **4)** ________________ or paralysing dose to the particular quarry of each venomous animal. Although the main purpose of venomous **5)** ________________ is to kill an animal's prey, some animals also to use it as a method of defence. The range of animals with a venomous **6)** ________________ is wide: many snakes, invertebrates, fish, and reptiles have the ability to bite, sting or stab their victims to **7)** ________________ the toxin. Snakes have **8)** ________________ , as do spiders and some fish. Other animals, such as centipedes, scorpions, bees, wasps, and some fish, sting their victims. The reaction of humans to animal venom varies. Bee and wasp stings are seldom fatal, unless the victim suffers from a serious **9)** ________________ reaction, called anaphylaxis. Snake and spider bites can be more serious but antivenoms are effective, provided they are **10)** ________________ soon after.

Score [ ] **Percentage** [%]

Cloze Activity Test 14

Fill in the missing letters to complete the passage.

As round their **1)** d _ i n _ father's bed

His sons attend, the **2)** p e _ s a _ t said:

"Children, deep hid from **3)** p _ y i n _ eyes,

A **4)** _ r e a s _ r _ in my vineyard lies;

When you have laid me in the **5)** g r _ v _ ,

Dig, search—and your **6)** r _ w a _ d you'll have."

"Father," cries one, "but where's the spot?"

He sighs! he **7)** s _ n k _ ! he answers not.

The **8)** t e _ i o _ s burial service over,

Home go his sons, and **9)** _ t r a i _ h _ explore

Each corner of the **10)** v _ n e _ a r d round,

Dig up, beat, break, and **11)** s _ f t the ground;

Yet though to search so well **12)** i n c _ i n e _ ,

Nor gold, nor treasure could they find;

But when the **13)** [a][ ][t][u][ ][n] next drew near,

A double **14)** [v][ ][n][t][a][g][ ] crowned the year.

"Now," **15)** [q][ ][o][t][h] the peasant's wisest son,

"Our father's **16)** [l][ ][g][a][ ][y] is known,

In yon rich **17)** [ ][u][r][p][ ][e] grapes 'tis seen,

Which, but for **18)** [d][ ][g][g][i][ ][g], never had been.

Then let us all **19)** [r][e][ ][l][e][c][ ] with pleasure.

That **20)** [l][ ][b][o][ ][r] is the source of treasure."

The Father's Treasure by Anon.

Score [ ] **Percentage** [%]

Cloze Activity Test 15

Choose the correct words from the word bank below to complete the passage.

tubing	**topics**	**essential**	**projection**	**paramount**
structures	**derived**	**scanning**	**membrane**	**mechanical**

The word "acoustic" is **1)** _______________ from the Greek word *akoustikos*, meaning "of or for hearing, ready to hear". Acoustics is the study of all **2)** _______________ waves in liquids, gases and solids and includes **3)** _______________ such as sound, vibration, ultrasound and infrasound. The science of acoustics covers many subjects including music, architecture, medicine, the workplace, industrial production, and even warfare. Knowledge of acoustics is **4)** _______________ when designing musical instruments. How the strings on a violin, the effect of the length of **5)** _______________ in a brass instrument, and the shape of a drum **6)** _______________ affect the performance of an acoustic instrument is of **7)** _______________ importance to their design. The design, choice of materials, and construction of a theatre or music hall must be sympathetic to the quality and **8)** _______________ of sound within the auditorium. In medicine, acoustics are used in developing ultrasound **9)** _______________ . Acoustic location uses sound to determine the distance and direction of something. It may take place in liquids, gases or solids, so may be used to measure the depth of the oceans, the distance of objects in space, or to find objects or **10)** _______________ deep underground.

Score ☐ **Percentage**

Cloze Activity Test 16

Fill in the missing letters to complete the passage.

When I was sick and lay a-bed,

I had two **1)** p _ l l _ w s at my head,

And all my toys **2)** b e _ i d _ me lay,

To keep me happy all the day.

And sometimes for an hour or so

I watched my leaden **3)** s _ l d _ e r _ go,

With different **4)** _ n i f _ r _ s and drills,

Among the bed-clothes, through the hills;

And **5)** s o _ e t _ m _ s sent my ships in fleets

All up and down among the sheets;

Or **6)** b _ o u _ h _ my trees and houses out,

And **7)** _ l a n t _ d cities all about.

I was the **8)** g _ _ n t great and still

That sits upon the pillow-hill,

And sees before him, **9)** d _ l e and plain,

The pleasant land of **10)** c o _ n t _ r p _ n e.

The Land of Counterpane by Robert Louis Stevenson (1850-1894).

Score | **Percentage**

Cloze Activity Test 17

Select the correct words to complete the passage below.

It happened one day, about noon, going **1)** ☐ over ☐ among ☐ towards my boat, I was **2)** ☐ hardly ☐ exceedingly ☐ awkwardly surprised with the print of a man's **3)** ☐ naked ☐ pink ☐ gloved foot on the shore, which was very plain to be seen on the **4)** ☐ pebbles ☐ rocks ☐ sand . I stood like one thunderstruck, or as if I had seen an **5)** ☐ apparition ☐ elephant ☐ instant . I listened, I looked round me, but I could hear nothing, nor see anything; I went up to a **6)** ☐ rising ☐ low ☐ watery ground to look farther; I went up the shore and down the shore, but it was all one; I could see no other **7)** ☐ seaweed ☐ impression ☐ ship but that one. I went to it again to see if there were any more, and to **8)** ☐ cope ☐ struggle ☐ observe if it might not be my fancy; but there was no room for that, for there was **9)** ☐ not ☐ hidden ☐ exactly the print of a foot—toes, heel, and every part of a foot. How it came **10)** ☐ thither ☐ not ☐ around I knew not, nor could I in the least imagine; but after **11)** ☐ colourful ☐ innumerable ☐ innovative fluttering thoughts, like a man perfectly

12) ☐ rich ☐ ill ☐ confused and out of myself, I came home to my **13)** ☐ fortification ☐ sheltered ☐ classroom , not feeling, as we say, the ground I went on, but **14)** ☐ happy ☐ terrified ☐ ransomed to the last degree, looking behind me at every two or three steps, **15)** ☐ mistaking ☐ cutting ☐ hearing every bush and tree, and fancying every **16)** ☐ hill ☐ cave ☐ stump at a distance to be a man. Nor is it possible to **17)** ☐ conscript ☐ decant ☐ describe how many various shapes my **18)** ☐ purple ☐ affrighted ☐ skeletal imagination represented things to me in, how many wild ideas were found every moment in my **19)** ☐ fancy ☐ pocket ☐ throat , and what strange, unaccountable **20)** ☐ tastes ☐ rushes ☐ whimsies came into my thoughts by the way.

Extract from *The Life and Adventures of Robinson Crusoe*
by Daniel Defoe (1660-1731).

Score ☐ **Percentage** ☐ %

Cloze Activity Test 18

Fill in the missing letters to complete the passage.

The Highway Code was first published on 14th April 1931, and priced at just one penny and **1)** [_ o n t a _ n e _] only 18 pages of advice. It was produced in response to the **2)** [d i _ t u r _ i n _ l _] high death rate on Britain's roads. Although there were only 2.3 million vehicles on Britain's roads at the time, the lack of a **3)** [c o m _ u _ s o _ y] driving test contributed to the 7,000 deaths each year. The first edition urged road users to be careful and **4)** [_ o n s _ d e _ a t e] to others and to put safety first. An expanded, more complete version was published in 1934. It included information on road signs and the dangers of driving under the **5)** [i n _ l _ e n _ e] of alcohol. A further revised edition included advice on how to join and leave a motorway, the danger of **6)** [_ i r e _ n e _ s] , and the need for drivers to use the service areas to rest and to **7)** [s t _ e _ _ h] their legs. The 1978 edition added the Green Cross Code and advice on improved vehicle **8)** [s _ c u _ i _ y] was included. The Highway Code applies to animals, pedestrians, cyclists, motorcyclists, and drivers, and failure to comply with the **9)** [m _ n d _ t _ r y] rules is a criminal offence. Significantly, although the number of vehicles on Britain's roads has increased to over 30 million, the number of road deaths has fallen to around 2,000 **10)** [a _ n u a _ l _] .

Score [ ] **Percentage** [ ] %

Cloze Activity Test 19

Select the correct words to complete the passage below.

James Blundell, born in London in 1791, was an English obstetrician

1) [☐ renowned / ☐ recalled / ☐ repealed] for performing the first successful **2)** [☐ transcript / ☐ transformation / ☐ transfusion] of

human blood to a patient for **3)** [☐ treatment / ☐ blockage / ☐ prevention] of a haemorrhage. He had

4) [☐ advised / ☐ charged / ☐ witnessed] many of his patients dying in childbirth and **5)** [☐ chose / ☐ prayed / ☐ resolved] to

find a remedy. Blundell conducted experiments with animal blood transfusions using

a **6)** [☐ syringe / ☐ cylinder / ☐ funnel] . He also discovered that he could collect the blood from the

7) [☐ recipient / ☐ corpse / ☐ donor] in a container before transfusing it into the **8)** [☐ recipient / ☐ donor / ☐ receptacle] .

In 1829, Dr Blundell **9)** [☐ accepted / ☐ accomplished / ☐ aquired] the first blood transfusion between two

humans. During his life he also **10)** [☐ destroyed / ☐ divulged / ☐ devised] many instruments for the

transfusion of blood, many of which are still in use today.

Score ☐ **Percentage** ☐ %

Cloze Activity Test 20

Choose the correct words from the word bank below to complete the passage.

stomach	**villainous**	**acted**	**speculated**	**perpetrated**
theories	**inexplicably**	**stuffed**	**faked**	**confiscated**
revenue	**apprehended**	**knack**	**embarrass**	**befriended**
violent	**accomplices**	**exhumed**	**granted**	**Roundhead**

On 9th May 1671, an infamous crime was **1)** _______________ by the self-styled Colonel Thomas Blood. During the Civil War, this Irishman switched allegiances from Royalist to **2)** _______________ and became a Parliamentary supporter. During the war, he **3)** _______________ as a spy for Cromwell's army. Blood was given estates in Ireland for his services but they were **4)** _______________ when Charles II was restored to the throne. He was involved in many **5)** _______________ adventures, including attempted kidnap and working with dissident religious movements. The Colonel had the **6)** _______________ of disappearing and evading capture by government forces. In 1671, Blood attempted to steal the Crown Jewels from the Tower of London. Over several days, pretending to be a parson, he **7)** _______________ the King's Jewel Keeper, Talbot Edwards, with an offer for his fictitious nephew to marry Edwards' daughter, and thereby secure a sizable income. Later, he tricked Edwards into letting Blood and his two **8)** _______________ into the jewel room. Once inside, the jewel keeper was hit on the head with a mallet and, when he continued to struggle, he was bound, gagged and stabbed in the **9)** _______________ . Blood used the mallet to flatten St. Edwards Crown and hid it under his clerical cloak while his accomplice, Blood's brother-in-law Hunt, filed the Sceptre with the Cross in two (as it did not fit in their bag), while the third man, Parrot, **10)** _______________ the Sovereign's Orb down his trousers. The robbers were disturbed and tried to flee, but they were all **11)** _______________ . Blood refused to be questioned by anyone and demanded to speak to the King himself. **12)** _______________ , his request was granted and he was interviewed in private by the monarch. Although a wanted man with a price on his head for previous **13)** _______________ crimes, mysteriously, Blood was released after a short time. Furthermore, he was **14)** _______________ a royal free pardon, awarded an annual pension of £500, and his confiscated Irish estates were returned to him. It has been **15)** _______________ that Blood may have been working for the King, stealing the Crown Jewels to provide much needed **16)** _______________ for Charles II. Other **17)** _______________ are that he was being repaid for his spying, or that he knew things that could **18)** _______________ the crown. Blood died at his home in 1680 and was buried in the churchyard of St Margaret's Church near St. James's Park. It is believed that his body was **19)** _______________ by the authorities for confirmation: such was his reputation for trickery, it was suspected he might have **20)** _______________ his death and funeral.

Score **Percentage**

Cloze Activity Test 21

Fill in the missing letters to complete the passage below.

At 9.18am on 22nd April 1884 an earthquake, which became known as the Colchester earthquake or the Great English Earthquake, shook South East England. Its **1)** e _ i c _ n t _ e was the villages of Wivenhoe, Abberton, Langenhoe and Peldon. It measured 4.6 on the Richter scale, lasted for about 20 seconds, and the tremors were felt across England, and even in France and Belgium. The earthquake has been **2)** a _ t r i b _ t e _ with claiming 3 to 5 lives, although contemporary accounts dispute this. The Times reported damage "in the many villages in the **3)** n e _ g _ b o _ r h _ o d of Colchester", and, according to local newspapers, almost every building had been affected. The Masonry **4)** t _ m b _ e d off the tower of the medieval church in Langenhoe, crashing into the roof of the nave and chancel. The nearby rectory was also damaged. Many poor people were made homeless and a **5)** _ o n s i _ e r _ b l _ number of small craft were destroyed by the waves created by the seismic **6)** a _ t i _ i t _ .

Earthquakes are a rarity in England and the **7)** i n _ a b i _ a n t _ living in and around Colchester were terrified by the **8)** f e r _ _ i t _ of the earthquake. The cause of the earthquake is thought to have been a movement along a **9)** f a _ l _ in the ancient Palaeozoic rocks that **10)** u _ d _ r p _ n most of Essex.

Score ____ **Percentage** ____ %

Cloze Activity Test 22

Select the correct words to complete the passage below.

The Order of Companion of Honour may be **1)** ☐ bestowed ☐ piled ☐ laded upon persons who have given **2)** ☐ reduced ☐ conspicuous ☐ speedy national service and for whom the **3)** ☐ distinction ☐ road ☐ juncture is deemed to be the most **4)** ☐ expensive ☐ useless ☐ appropriate form of recognition. The Order was instituted in 1917 by King George V, in the same year as the **5)** ☐ future ☐ failures ☐ founding of the British Empire. At any time, the Order comprises the **6)** ☐ Sovereign ☐ Minister ☐ Headmaster and only 65 members, although foreigners may be admitted as honorary Companions.

7) ☐ Recipients ☐ Rascals ☐ Renegades are entitled to add 'CH' after their name. The Order's badge is a gold, oval-shaped **8)** ☐ certificate ☐ ribbon ☐ medallion with a representation of an oak tree. Its **9)** ☐ function ☐ price ☐ motto is "In action faithful and in honour clear." Recipients include artists, scientists, actors, poets, historians, **10)** ☐ politicians ☐ plumbers ☐ publicans and musicians.

Score ☐ **Percentage** ☐ %

Cloze Activity Test 23

Choose the correct words from the word bank below to complete the passage.

woody	**whitewashed**	**darkness**	**may**	**jockey**
cast	**disbeliever**	**trunks**	**clap**	**shaded**
bolted	**haunt**	**galloped**	**overtaken**	**beaming**
sunbeams	**encountered**	**foray**	**punch**	**turned**

The sequestered situation of this church seems always to have made it a favourite **1)** _______________ of troubled spirits. It stands on a knoll, surrounded by locust-trees and lofty elms, from among which its decent, **2)** _______________ walls shine modestly forth, like Christian purity **3)** _______________ through the shades of retirement. A gentle slope descends from it to a silver sheet of water, bordered by high trees, between which, peeps **4)** _______________ be caught at the blue hills of the Hudson. To look upon its grass-grown yard, where the **5)** _______________ seem to sleep so quietly, one would think that there at least the dead might rest in peace. On one side of the church extends a wide **6)** _______________ dell, along which raves a large brook among broken rocks and **7)** _______________ of fallen trees. Over a deep black part of the stream, not far from the church, was formerly thrown a wooden bridge; the road that led to it, and the bridge itself, were thickly **8)** _______________ by overhanging trees, which **9)** _______________ a gloom about it, even in the daytime; but occasioned a fearful **10)** _______________ at night. Such was one of the favourite haunts of the Headless Horseman, and the place where he was most frequently **11)** _______________ . The tale was told of old Brouwer, a most heretical **12)** _______________ in ghosts, how he met the Horseman returning from his **13)** _______________ into Sleepy Hollow, and was obliged to get up behind him; how they **14)** _______________ over bush and brake, over hill and swamp, until they reached the bridge; when the Horseman suddenly **15)** _______________ into a skeleton, threw old Brouwer into the brook, and sprang away over the tree-tops with a **16)** _______________ of thunder.

This story was immediately matched by a thrice marvellous adventure of Brom Bones, who made light of the Galloping Hessian as an arrant **17)** _______________ . He affirmed that on returning one night from the neighbouring village of Sing Sing, he had been **18)** _______________ by this midnight trooper; that he had offered to race with him for a bowl of **19)** _______________ , and should have won it too, for Daredevil beat the goblin horse all hollow, but just as they came to the church bridge, the Hessian **20)** _______________ , and vanished in a flash of fire.

Extract from *The Legend of Sleepy Hollow* by Washington Irvine (1783-1859).

Score [ ] **Percentage** [%]

Cloze Activity Test 24

Fill in the missing letters to complete the passage below.

On 21st October 1966, in the small mining village of Aberfan, South Wales, a most **1)** h _ r r _ w _ n g disaster occurred that took the lives of 116 children and 28 adults. At 9.15am, the children of Pantglas Junior School were returning to their classrooms after morning assembly. After several days of heavy rain, a build-up of rainwater in the **2)** a c c _ m u _ a t _ d rock and shale caused the colliery waste tip to suddenly slide downhill in an **3)** _ v a l a _ c h _ of slurry. Over 150,000 cubic metres of **4)** d e b _ _ s covered the village in minutes, **5)** e n _ u l _ i n _ the school and 20 houses. At the time, the village, **6)** _ e s t l _ _ g in the valley, was **7)** s _ r o _ d e _ in fog. The sound of the impending disaster could be heard as the enormous volume of earth and coal waste thundered towards the village. Almost 2,000 volunteers rushed to the scene in a **8)** _ r a _ t _ c rescue operation, but they were powerless to prevent the tragic loss of life. In 1958, the tip had been sited on a known stream and had previously suffered several minor slips. Its **9)** _ n s t a _ i l _ t y was known both to colliery management and to tip workers, but very little was done about it. The National Coal Board was heavily **10)** c _ i t i _ i s e _ in the ensuing tribunal.

Score ☐ **Percentage** ☐ %

Cloze Activity Test 25

Select the correct words to complete the passage below.

Contrary to public **1)** [ ] misconception / [ ] footpaths / [ ] fascination , Henry Ford (1863-1947) invented neither the motor car nor the assembly line. He did, however, manufacture the first **2)** [ ] wheeled / [ ] green / [ ] affordable motor car, the Model T, and make it a practical **3)** [ ] conveyance / [ ] joke / [ ] solution . He is credited with introducing a moving **4)** [ ] washing / [ ] assembly / [ ] white line that enabled a relatively unskilled worker to learn a simple, **5)** [ ] repetitive / [ ] difficult / [ ] expensive operation. Ford was a philanthropist, who was **6)** [ ] reluctant / [ ] destined / [ ] eager to ensure his employees were **7)** [ ] poorly / [ ] never / [ ] adequately rewarded with high wages. He became one of the richest people in the world and left most of his wealth to the Ford Foundation that is **8)** [ ] committed / [ ] beckoned / [ ] welded to programmes that strengthen **9)** [ ] low / [ ] property / [ ] democratic values, reduce poverty and **10)** [ ] temperatures / [ ] criticism / [ ] injustice , and advance human knowledge, creativity and achievement.

Score [ ] **Percentage**

Cloze Activity Test 26

Choose the correct words from the word bank below to complete the passage.

suffix	**increased**	**plaques**	**respectively**	**revolutionary**
tension	**portrayed**	**identical**	**proportions**	**constitutes**
evolved	**popular**	**debatable**	**superseded**	**obviated**
sharply	**resembles**	**gradually**	**counterparts**	**construction**

The oldest iconic representation of a stringed instrument is **1)** ______________ in a stone carving which is more than 3,300 years old. An instrument that bears a strong resemblance to a guitar is illustrated in Babylonian clay **2)** ______________ , so it may be that the origin of the guitar predates 12th Century chordophones. There are five basic types of chordophones, which were developed across Europe: bows, harps, lutes, lyres, and zithers, of which the lute most closely **3)** ______________ a guitar. One of the earliest of these is a long-necked lute, either Roman or Byzantine, from Egypt. The lute has a waisted soundbox (or body) like a guitar and was **4)** ______________ from the third to sixth century. The vihuela, which dates from the 14th to the 17th century, is larger than a guitar, has six or seven doubled strings (paired courses) and is tuned like a lute. Some illustrations show it with a **5)** ______________ cut waist, similar to a violin, while others show rounded corners more like a guitar. Both the vihuela and the guitar coexisted until the 17th century, when the guitar's popularity **6)** ______________ that of the vihuela. The last surviving music for the vihuela was published in 1576. The definition of exactly what **7)** ______________ a guitar is given as having "a long, fretted neck, flat wooden soundboard, ribs, and a flat back, most often with incurved sides". The modern English word "guitar" and its French and German **8)** ______________ , "guitare" and "Gitarre" **9)** ______________ , are derived from the Spanish "guitarra". This word comes from the Andalusian Arabic "quitara". The 10) _______________ , "tar" is the ancient Sanskrit word for "string". The prefix denotes the number of strings: *dotar* – two strings; *setar* – three strings; *chartar* – four strings. The four-course "chitarra" was **11)** _______________ replaced by the five-course "guitarra battente", which had a standard tuning **12)** _______________ to the top five strings of a modern-day guitar. Over time, the neck length from the instrument's body was **13)** _______________ from 8 frets to 10 frets, then to 12 frets. In the 17th century, the Italians added a sixth course of strings, which finally **14)** _______________ into six single strings. In 1850, the Spanish luthier, Antonio Torres, redesigned the guitar and introduced the **15)** _______________ "fan- top" bracing pattern. To improve the volume, tone and projection of the instrument, the size and **16)** _______________ of the body were altered. The classical guitar has since remained essentially unchanged to this day. Around 1900, the advent of steel strings presented the opportunity to build louder guitars. However, the fan-braced top of classical guitars was not capable of withstanding the increased **17)** _______________ of steel strings. X-braced tops, first developed by a German immigrant to the USA, Christian Fredrich Martin, became the industry standard for the **18)** _______________ of steel strung flat-top guitars. In the late 1920s, with the advent of amplification, pick-ups were added to jazz guitars. This **19)** _______________ the need for a hollow body, giving rise to the construction of solid body electric guitars. The creator of the first solid bodied guitar is **20)** _______________ but, from its humble beginnings, the guitar has evolved into one of the most popular instruments of choice.

Score | | **Percentage** | %

Cloze Activity Test 27

Select the correct words to complete the passage below.

She lingered, and resisted my **1)** [☐ persuasions ☐ sights ☐ persuant] to departure a tiresome while; but as he neither looked up nor spoke, she finally made a **2)** [☐ shout ☐ handle ☐ movement] to the door, and I followed. We were recalled by a **3)** [☐ scream ☐ cloud ☐ soldier]. Linton had slid from his seat on to the hearthstone, and lay **4)** [☐ comfortably ☐ crawling ☐ writhing] in the mere perverseness of an indulged plague of a child, determined to be as **5)** [☐ grievous ☐ still ☐ conscious] and harassing as it can. I thoroughly **6)** [☐ smelled ☐ stunned ☐ gauged] his disposition from his behaviour, and saw at once it would be **7)** [☐ stutter ☐ rich ☐ folly] to attempt humouring him. Not so my **8)** [☐ companion ☐ brother ☐ horse]: she ran back in terror, **9)** [☐ rolled ☐ stood ☐ knelt] down, and cried, and soothed, and entreated, till he grew quiet from lack of **10)** [☐ breath ☐ food ☐ fears]: by no means from compunction at distressing her.

Extract from *Wuthering Heights* by Emily Brontë (1818-1848).

Score ☐ **Percentage** ☐ %

Cloze Activity Test 28

Fill in the missing letters to complete the passage below.

Standing only 4ft 10in, the diminutive Helena Rubinstein was born in 1884. When she **1)** e m _ g r _ t _ d from her native Poland to Australia in 1902 she had no money and little English. However, her **2)** s t _ l i _ _ clothes and milky-white **3)** c _ m p l e _ i o _ did not go unnoticed and she found a ready market for the jars of beauty cream in her luggage. She decided to **4)** _ a n u _ a c t u _ e her own, using lanolin extracted from sheep's wool with essence of lavender, pine bark or water lilies added to disguise the **5)** p _ n g _ n t odour. She was "the first self-made female millionaire", an **6)** a c _ o m _ l i _ h _ e n t she owed primarily to publicity savvy. She knew how to advertise—using 'fear copy with a bit of blah-blah'—and introduced the **7)** c _ n _ e p _ of 'problem' skin types. She also pioneered the use of pseudoscience in marketing, **8)** d _ n n i _ g a lab coat in many advertisements, despite the fact that her only training had been a two-month tour of European skin-care facilities. She knew how to manipulate consumers' status anxiety, as well: If a product **9)** f _ l t _ r e _ initially, she would hike the price to raise the **10)** p e _ c e i v _ d value. She died a multi-millionaire in 1965.

Score | **Percentage** %

Cloze Activity Test 29

Choose the correct words from the word bank below to complete the passage.

giggles	**gentleman**	**rude**	**terrible**	**matters**
bade	**disgrace**	**tilts**	**dinner**	**fidgety**
snapped	**cloth**	**able**	**bare**	**tumbling**
fret	**grave**	**fairly**	**swings**	**child**

'Let me see if Philip can

Be a little **1)** _______________ ;

Let me see if he is **2)** _______________

To sit still for once at table:'

Thus Papa **3)** _______________ Phil behave;

And Mamma looked very **4)** _______________ .

But **5)** _______________ Phil,

He won't sit still;

He wriggles,

And **6)** _______________ ,

And then, I declare,

7) _______________ backwards and forwards,

And **8)** _______________ up his chair,

Just like any rocking-horse

'Philip! I am getting cross!'

See the naughty, restless **9)** _______________

Growing still more **10)** _______________ and wild,

Till his chair falls over quite.

Philip screams with all his might,

Catches at the **11)** _______________ , but then

That makes **12)** _______________ worse again.

Down upon the ground they fall,

Glasses, plates, knives, forks, and all.

How Mamma did **13)** _______________ and frown,

When she saw them **14)** _______________ down!

And Papa made such a face!

Philip is in sad **15)** _______________ .

Where is Philip, where is he?

16) _______________ covered up you see!

Cloth and all are lying on him;

He has pulled down all upon him.

What a **17)** _______________ to-do!

Dishes, glasses, **18)** _______________ in two!

Here a knife, and there a fork!

Philip, this is cruel work.

Table all so **19)** _______________ , and ah!

Poor Papa, and poor Mamma

Look quite cross, and wonder how

They shall have their **20)** _______________ now.

The Story of Fidgety Philip
by Heinrich Hoffmann (1809-1894).

Score [ ] **Percentage** [%]

Cloze Activity Test 30

Fill in the missing letters to complete the passage below.

María Eva Duarte de Perón was born in 1919 in **1)** [r _ r _ l] Argentina. She is usually referred to as Eva Perón, or by the affectionate Spanish language **2)** [d i _ i n _ t i _ e], Evita. At the age of 15, she moved to Buenos Aires to pursue a career on the stage and radio, but she had to survive without **3)** [_ o r m _ l] education or connections. Eventually, she was **4)** [c _ n t _ a c _ e d] to the biggest radio station, and by 1943 she was one of the highest paid radio actresses in Argentina. Her success gave her sufficient financial **5)** [s _ a b _ l i _ y] to enable her to move into her own apartment in the most exclusive area of Buenos Aires. Eva Duarte's husband, Juan Perón, was Minister of Labour and had **6)** [c o _ s i _ e r _ b l _] support from the army and the country. Perón was arrested and imprisoned by his opponents in the government but was released six days later as a result of public **7)** [_ e _ o n _ t _ a t _ o n s]. When he stood for president, in 1946, Eva delivered powerful speeches in his support on her radio show and he won a **8)** [l a _ d s _ i d _] victory. In 1947, unaccompanied by her husband, Eva embarked on the '*Rainbow Tour*' of Europe, meeting with various **9)** [d i _ n i _ a r i _ s] and heads of state. When Eva died in 1952 at the age of 33, Argentina went into **10)** [_ o u r _ i n _].

Score [ ] **Percentage** [%]

Cloze Activity Test 31

Fill in the missing letters to complete the passage below.

We were not too soon, for just as we reached **1)** [s][h][ ][l][ ][e][ ] the sun went down with startling **2)** [r][a][ ][i][d][ ][t][y], leaving the world nearly dark, for in these latitudes there is but little **3)** [ ][w][ ][l][i][g][ ][t]. So we crept into the cave, which did not appear to be very big, and **4)** [h][u][ ][d][l][ ][n][g] ourselves together for warmth, swallowed what remained of our brandy—barely a mouthful each—and tried to forget our **5)** [m][ ][s][ ][r][i][ ][s] in sleep. But the cold was too intense to allow us to do so, for I am convinced that at this great **6)** [a][l][ ][i][t][u][ ][e] the thermometer cannot have marked less than fourteen or fifteen degrees below freezing point. What such a temperature meant to us, enervated as we were by hardship, want of food, and the great heat of the desert, the reader may imagine better than I can describe. **7)** [S][ ][f][f][i][ ][e] it to say that it was something as near death from **8)** [e][ ][p][ ][s][u][r][ ] as I have ever felt. There we sat hour after hour through the still and bitter night, feeling the frost wander round and nip us now in the finger, now in the foot, now in the face. In **9)** [v][ ][i][ ] did we huddle up closer and closer; there was no warmth in our miserable starved **10)** [c][a][ ][c][ ][s][e][ ]. Sometimes one of us would drop into an uneasy slumber for a few minutes, but we could not sleep much, and perhaps this was fortunate, for if we had I doubt if we should have ever woke again.

Extract from *King Solomon's Mines*
by H. Rider Haggard (1856-1929).

Score [ ] **Percentage** [%]

Cloze Activity Test 32

Select the correct words to complete the passage below.

Horatio Nelson was born in Norfolk in 1758. At the age of 12 he joined, as an

1) ☐ ordinary / ☐ merchant / ☐ experienced seaman and coxswain, the ship *HMS Raisonnable* under the

2) ☐ commital / ☐ comment / ☐ command of his maternal uncle. He was appointed a midshipman shortly

after and began his officer training. He rose rapidly through the **3)** ☐ ranks / ☐ rigging / ☐ air and

achieved his own command in 1778. He **4)** ☐ benefitted / ☐ shrank / ☐ suffered from seasickness

throughout his entire naval career and from several recurring **5)** ☐ bites / ☐ bouts / ☐ bales of

malaria. During a year spent at home in 1783/4, Nelson **6)** ☐ contemplated / ☐ resisted / ☐ concocted

standing for Parliament but was unable to find a seat. He was given command of the

7) ☐ frigate / ☐ lifeboat / ☐ submarine *HMS Boreas* in 1784 and **8)** ☐ stoked / ☐ repaired / ☐ set sail for Antigua. Whilst

there, he met and married Francis Nisbet in 1787 in Nevis, a small

9) ☐ mountain / ☐ island / ☐ oasis in the Caribbean Sea. They returned to England and

10) ☐ settled / ☐ secured / ☐ secluded in Nelson's home town of Thorpe in Norfolk. He was now in

11) ☐ contention / ☐ prison / ☐ reserve, on half pay and **12)** ☐ reluctant / ☐ desperate / ☐ sad to be given another

command. Unfortunately, in the **13)** ☐ French / ☐ expanding / ☐ peacetime navy there were too few ships

available. He was **14)** ☐ recalled / ☐ collected / ☐ prised to be captain of the 64-gun *HMS Agamemnon* in

January 1793, just one month before France **15)** ☐ deployed / ☐ deluded / ☐ declared war. In 1794, Nelson

lost the sight in his right eye after being **16)** ☐ wounded / ☐ inspected / ☐ abandoned in Corsica and lost his

right arm at the Battle of Santa Cruz de Tenerife in 1797. Nelson was

17) ☐ appointed / ☐ celebrated / ☐ conscripted commander-in-chief of the Mediterranean Fleet and took

18) ☐ notice / ☐ command / ☐ cover of his most famous ship, *HMS Victory*, in 1803. At the Battle

of Trafalgar in 1805, Nelson was **19)** ☐ seriously / ☐ slightly / ☐ mortally wounded by a shot from an

enemy sniper. His body was returned to England to be **20)** ☐ exhibited / ☐ exhumed / ☐ interred in

St Paul's Cathedral.

Score ☐ **Percentage** ☐ %

Cloze Activity Test 33

Fill in the missing letters to complete the passage below.

Spring opened late that year, but the Summer, when it came, was a warm one. Katy felt the heat very much. She could not change her seat and follow the **1)** b _ e e _ e about from window to window as other people could. The long burning days left her weak and **2)** p a _ c h e _ . She hung her head, and seemed to **3)** _ i l t like the flowers in the garden-beds. Indeed she was worse off than they, for every evening Alexander gave them a watering with the hose, while nobody was able to bring a watering-pot and pour out what she needed – a shower of cold, fresh air. It wasn't easy to be good-humoured under these **4)** _ i r c _ m s _ a _ c e _ , and one could hardly have blamed Katy if she had sometimes forgotten her **5)** r _ s o _ u t _ _ n _ and been cross and **6)** f r _ t f _ l . But she didn't – not very often. Now and then bad days came, when she was discouraged and **7)** f _ r l _ _ n . But Katy's long year of schooling had taught her self-control, and, as a general thing, her **8)** d i _ c o _ _ o r _ s were borne patiently. She could not help growing pale and thin, however, and Papa saw with concern that, as the summer went on, she became too **9)** l _ n g _ i _ to read, or study, or sew, and just sat hour after hour, with folded hands, **10)** g _ z _ n _ wistfully out of the window.

Extract from *What Katy Did*
by Susan Coolidge (1835-1905).

Score [ ] **Percentage** [%]

Cloze Activity Test 34

Choose the correct words from the word bank below to complete the passage.

gained	**circumnavigate**	**leg**	**cropped**	**determined**
altitude	**aviators**	**airfield**	**fund**	**contended**

Amelia Mary Earhart was born on July 24, 1897. When she was 23 years old, she and her father visited an **1)** _______________ and she was taken up in an aircraft for a ten minute flight that would change her life. After that flight she said, "I knew I had to fly." She became **2)** _______________ to learn to fly and worked in a variety of jobs to **3)** _______________ her lessons. She purchased a leather flying jacket and had her hair **4)** _______________ short in the style of female **5)** _______________ of the time. She purchased a second-hand, bright yellow biplane, which she nicknamed *The Canary*. Even before she **6)** _______________ her pilot's licence, she set a women's world **7)** _______________ record, taking *The Canary* up to 14,000 feet. At the age of 34, Earhart began to attempt the first solo flight by a female pilot across the Atlantic. She took off from Harbour Grace, Newfoundland, taking with her a copy of the *Telegraph-Journal* dated 20th May, 1932, to confirm the date of the attempt, intending to land in Paris. After a flight lasting 14 hours, 56 minutes during which she **8)** _______________ with strong northerly winds, icy conditions and mechanical problems, Earhart landed in a field at Culmore, north of Derry, Northern Ireland. In 1937, Earhart and her crew member, Fred Noonan, began their attempt to **9)** _______________ the globe. Having completed 22,000 miles they set off to cross the Pacific on the final **10)** _______________ but the aircraft disappeared. The two bodies and their aircraft were never recovered.

Score [ ] **Percentage**

Cloze Activity Test 35

Select the correct words to complete the passage below.

We walk past them every day; they have **1)** ☐ polluted / ☐ granted / ☐ graced our streets for over 150 years; their use and necessity has not changed in all that time. It is **2)** ☐ estimated / ☐ censored / ☐ contorted that there are over 100,000 **3)** ☐ searching / ☐ stalling / ☐ surviving red post boxes in the United Kingdom. This number includes the **4)** ☐ unsighted / ☐ ubiquitous / ☐ uncertain red pillar box, with a black base, wall boxes and lamp boxes. The latter are **5)** ☐ mounted / ☐ missing / ☐ mailed on a post. They may also be found all over the world in most **6)** ☐ fastidious / ☐ worthy / ☐ former nations of the British Empire, members of the Commonwealth of Nations and British **7)** ☐ overseas / ☐ local / ☐ ancient territories. The first pillar boxes were **8)** ☐ excreted / ☐ excluded / ☐ erected in St. Helier, Jersey in 1852, just 12 years after the introduction of the **9)** ☐ expensive / ☐ useless / ☐ uniform penny post and the penny black, which was the first **10)** ☐ ad hoc / ☐ adhesive / ☐ addressed postage stamp. These pillar boxes were painted green and it was not until 1874 that the now **11)** ☐ familiar / ☐ faded / ☐ feasible red hue was adopted. On the

12) ☐ contrary ☐ rebound ☐ mainland , the first pillar boxes were **13)** ☐ installed ☐ stolen ☐ damaged in Carlisle in 1853, with London having to wait a further two years before five were placed in the **14)** ☐ provinces ☐ countryside ☐ capital . Since 1905, the traditional **15)** ☐ cylindrical ☐ pygmy ☐ octagonal pillar boxes are made of cast iron. In more recent times, pillar boxes found in secure indoor locations, such as **16)** ☐ carparks ☐ footpaths ☐ supermarkets and shopping malls, are constructed from glass fibre or plastic. Each pillar box has a **17)** ☐ unique ☐ bent ☐ clear Chubb lock with its individual key. There are no **18)** ☐ stubby ☐ skeleton ☐ bright keys and postal workers have to carry a **19)** ☐ clutch ☐ gaggle ☐ bunch of keys with them to **20)** ☐ empty ☐ fill ☐ chase all the boxes on their round.

Score ☐ **Percentage** 

Cloze Activity Test 36

Choose the correct words from the word bank below to complete the passage.

scarce	**struck**	**throb**	**haul**	**bewilderment**
giddy	**clutched**	**violently**	**tugged**	**clambering**

In a moment I was **1)** _______________ by several hands, and there was no mistaking that they were trying to **2)** _______________ me back. I struck another light, and waved it in their dazzled faces. You can **3)** _______________ imagine how nauseatingly inhuman they looked - those pale, chinless faces and great, lidless, pinkish-grey eyes! - as they stared in their blindness and **4)** _______________ . But I did not stay to look, I promise you: I retreated again, and when my second match had ended, I **5)** _______________ my third. It had almost burned through when I reached the opening into the shaft. I lay down on the edge, for the **6)** _______________ of the great pump below made me **7)** _______________ . Then I felt sideways for the projecting hooks, and, as I did so, my feet were grasped from behind, and I was violently **8)** _______________ backward. I lit my last match ... and it incontinently went out. But I had my hand on the climbing bars now, and, kicking **9)** _______________ , I disengaged myself from the clutches of the Morlocks and was speedily **10)** _______________ up the shaft, while they stayed peering and blinking up at me: all but one little wretch who followed me for some way, and well nigh secured my boot as a trophy.

Extract from *The Time Machine* by H. G. Wells (1866-1946).

Score ☐ **Percentage** ☐ %

Cloze Activity Test 37

Fill in the missing letters to complete the passage below.

The rooks are **1)** b u _ l d i n _ on the trees;

They build there every **2)** s _ r i n _ :

"Caw, caw," is all they say,

For none of them can sing.

They're up before the break of day,

And up till late at night;

For they must **3)** l a _ o u _ busily

As long as it is **4)** l i _ _ t .

And many a **5)** c _ o o k _ d stick they bring,

And many a slender **6)** _ w _ g ,

And many a **7)** t _ f t of moss, until

Their nests are round and big.

"Caw, caw!" Oh, what a noise

They make in **8)** _ a i n _ weather!

Good children always **9)** s _ e a k by turns,

But rooks all talk **10)** _ o g _ t h _ r .

The Rooks by Jane Euphemia Browne (1811-1898).

Score [ ] **Percentage** [%]

Cloze Activity Test 38

Choose the correct words from the word bank below to complete the passage.

auspices	**contracting**	**solidarity**	**safety**	**concealed**
smuggle	**tolerated**	**creating**	**permit**	**accomplices**
pretext	**codename**	**execution**	**typhus**	**ingenious**
nominated	**tortured**	**enormous**	**honours**	**occupation**

Irena Sendler was born as Irena Krzyżanowska in 1910 near Warsaw in Poland. Her father, Dr. Stanisław Krzyżanowski, was a doctor and died from **1)** _______________ he contracted while treating patients other doctors refused to treat for fear of **2)** _______________ the disease; among them many were Jews. After her father's death, Jewish leaders offered to help her mother pay for Irena's education.

During the German **3)** _______________ of Poland in World War II, Irena lived in Warsaw. She was employed by the Social Welfare Department and was given a special **4)** _______________ to enter the Warsaw Ghetto to check for signs of typhus. The occupying army feared the disease would spread beyond the Ghetto.

She began aiding Jews soon after the German invasion in 1939. In August 1943, Irena, known by her nom de guerre: '*Jolanta*', was **5)** _______________ by Żegota to head its Jewish children's section. She led a group of co-workers to help Jewish families by **6)** _______________ more than 3,000 false documents for them.

Żegota was the **7)** _______________ for The Council to Aid Jews, which operated under the **8)** _______________ of the Polish Government in Exile. The organisation, the only one of its kind in any country in Nazi-occupied Europe, helped the country's Jews and found places of **9)** _______________ for them in occupied Poland. Irena worked with a group of about thirty volunteers, who were mostly women.

Assisting the Jewish community in any way was extremely dangerous and undertaken at **10)** ________________ risk. Not only was the person involved threatened with the death penalty, but so were their entire family or household. It was only in Poland where such action was punishable by death.

The main purpose of the organisation was to **11)** ________________ babies and small children out of the Ghetto. This was achieved using ambulances and trams and by using other **12)** ________________ methods: babies were even **13)** ________________ in packages, tool boxes and suitcases. The rescued children were placed with Polish families, orphanages and convents. By cooperating with the RGO, which was a Polish relief organisation **14)** ________________ by the occupying forces, Irena visited the Ghetto under the **15)** ________________ of inspecting sanitary conditions. During these visits, Irena wore a Star of David as a sign of **16)** ________________ with the Jewish people and so as not to draw attention to herself.

In 1943, the Gestapo arrested and severely **17)** ________________ Irena. They beat her brutally, fracturing her feet and legs. Her refusal to betray any of her **18)** ________________ , or the children they rescued, resulted in her being sentenced to death by firing squad. She was saved from this fate when Żegota bribed the guards on the way to her **19)** ________________ .

After the war Irena was awarded numerous **20)** ________________ ; among them was the Nobel Peace Prize in 2009.

Irena Sendler died in Warsaw on 12 May 2008, aged 98.

Score [ ] **Percentage**

Cloze Activity Test 39

Select the correct words to complete the passage below.

Perhaps the first use of forensic science may be **1)** [ ] attributed [ ] rushed [ ] alluded to Archimedes. He was asked to **2)** [ ] ascertain [ ] try [ ] gamble whether a goldsmith had **3)** [ ] manufactured [ ] polished [ ] substituted silver for pure gold he used to make a crown for King Hiero II. Archimedes **4)** [ ] overcame [ ] compounded [ ] strained the problem of how this could be achieved without having to melt down the crown to measure the **5)** [ ] frequency [ ] length [ ] density of the material. Instead, he **6)** [ ] preserved [ ] busted [ ] repealed the undamaged crown by using the law of displacement to prove the goldsmith's dishonesty. Forensic science covers a multitude of **7)** [ ] sins [ ] disciplines [ ] descendants including toxicology and ballistics, anthropometry, fingerprinting, photography and many others. **8)** [ ] Modern [ ] Dismal [ ] Caustic forensic science dates from the 18th century when **9)** [ ] conscious [ ] crowded [ ] criminal investigation became a more evidence-based, **10)** [ ] random [ ] raucous [ ] rational procedure. Prior to this, extreme measures, such as using torture to extract

11) [☐ complaints / ☐ converts / ☐ confessions] , and belief in the power of the occult and witchcraft

12) [☐ gained / ☐ cursed / ☐ used] to influence the court's decisions. In 1784, forensic evidence in the

trial of John Toms led to his **13)** [☐ conviction / ☐ passion / ☐ eviction] for murder. Newspaper found in the

head wound of the victim matched that **14)** [☐ enterred / ☐ leaking / ☐ found] in Toms' pocket. It had

been used by Toms to make a pistol wad in the weapon he used to **15)** [☐ shoot / ☐ stab / ☐ stifle] his

victim. In 1858, fingerprinting to **16)** [☐ identify / ☐ annoy / ☐ allude] criminal suspects was

17) [☐ busted / ☐ poached / ☐ advocated] by Sir William Herschel, who worked for the Indian Civil Service

and used **18)** [☐ elbow / ☐ knee / ☐ thumb] prints on documents to prove their

19) [☐ heritage / ☐ authenticity / ☐ usefulness] . More recently, in 1984, the scientist Alec Jeffreys

20) [☐ pioneered / ☐ banned / ☐ pretended] the use of DNA profiling in forensic science.

Score ☐ **Percentage** ☐ %

Cloze Activity Test 40

Choose the correct words from the word bank below to complete the passage.

developed	**communicate**	**impaired**	**advocate**	**frustrated**
contracted	**breakthrough**	**directed**	**activist**	**vocabulary**

When she was born in Alabama in 1880, Helen Keller's sight and hearing were normal. When she was 19 months old she **1)** ________________ an illness, thought to be scarlet fever or meningitis, which left her deaf and blind. She began to use signs to **2)** ________________ , and the family cook's six-year-old daughter was able to understand them. Helen **3)** ________________ these signs and, by the time she was seven, she had a **4)** "________________" of more than 60, which she used in the family home. Helen's mother sought help for her daughter and was **5)** ________________ to the Perkins Institute for the Blind. 20-year-old Anne Sullivan, a former pupil of the Institute, who was herself visually **6)** ________________ , became Helen's instructor. She began to spell words onto Helen's hand, beginning with "d-o-l-l", for the doll she had given her as a present. Not understanding that every object had a name, Helen became extremely **7)** ________________ . The **8)** ________________ came when Anne ran water over one of Helen's hands while spelling out the word on the other. Helen Keller became a political **9)** ________________ and a world famous speaker. She died in 1968 and is remembered as an **10)** ________________ for people with disabilities.

Score [ ] **Percentage** [%]

Answers

Test 1
1) rose
2) brink
3) barley
4) float
5) swan
6) Sailing
7) mellow
8) flowers
9) clouds
10) twilight

Test 2
1) founder
2) pursued
3) lifting
4) promoted
5) revered
6) learnt
7) manual
8) organisations
9) suit
10) ideas
11) instalments
12) approximately
13) en route
14) engaged
15) sensation
16) donated
17) Jamboree
18) acclaimed
19) bears
20) trail

Test 3
1) original
2) credited
3) efficiency
4) ingenuity
5) employed
6) adaptation
7) hauled
8) aptitude
9) bankrupt
10) exploit

Test 4
1) nickname
2) knowledge
3) carried
4) criminal
5) experience
6) enlisted
7) rigging
8) travelling
9) sorted
10) stole

Test 5
1) prototypes
2) treaty
3) equivalent
4) aspirations
5) technological
6) maiden
7) supersonic
8) mankind
9) inclement
10) observed
11) instrumentation
12) thundered
13) spontaneous
14) visibility
15) manually
16) uneventfully
17) inoperative
18) withdrawn
19) magnificent
20) genius

Test 6
1) reserves
2) prospecting
3) relied
4) consumption
5) commence
6) provided
7) swelled
8) coffers
9) extracted
10) conclusion

Test 7
1) courted
2) churches
3) rode
4) buttercups
5) cats
6) worried
7) baby
8) crown
9) world
10) blunders

Test 8
1) unpleasant
2) disagreeable
3) abhorred
4) liberty
5) hesitate
6) irritated
7) humane
8) berated
9) sarcastic
10) rector
11) circumstances
12) pressing
13) dreaded
14) villainous
15) retailed

Answers

16) honest
17) village
18) intimate
19) language
20) agreeable

Test 9
1) discoveries
2) complained
3) sour
4) growth
5) patented
6) pursue
7) immunising
8) trial
9) mauled
10) popularly

Test 10
1) diseases
2) developed
3) established
4) husbandry
5) thoroughly
6) sufficient
7) microbes
8) utensils
9) sterilising
10) germs

Test 11
1) consideration
2) generator
3) extraction
4) commercial
5) plant
6) invented
7) granted
8) implemented
9) drawn
10) sustainable
11) capacity
12) utlise
13) heated
14) imports
15) polluted
16) crust
17) decaying
18) conduction
19) natural
20) active

Test 12
1) skilful
2) plain
3) halt
4) prostration
5) stupefied
6) effects
7) fumes
8) disturbed
9) fate
10) inevitably

Test 13
1) sting
2) evolved
3) predator
4) lethal
5) toxins
6) capability
7) inject
8) fangs
9) allergic
10) administered

Test 14
1) dying
2) peasant
3) prying
4) treasure
5) grave
6) reward
7) sinks
8) tedious
9) straight
10) vineyard
11) sift
12) inclined
13) autumn
14) vintage
15) quoth
16) legacy
17) purple
18) digging
19) reflect
20) labour

Test 15
1) derived
2) mechanical
3) topics
4) essential
5) tubing
6) membrane
7) paramount
8) projection
9) scanning
10) structures

Test 16
1) pillows
2) beside
3) soldiers
4) uniforms
5) sometimes
6) brought
7) planted
8) giant
9) dale
10) counterpane

Answers

Test 17
1) towards
2) exceedingly
3) naked
4) sand
5) apparition
6) rising
7) impression
8) observe
9) exactly
10) thither
11) innumerable
12) confused
13) fortification
14) terrified
15) mistaking
16) stump
17) describe
18) affrighted
19) fancy
20) whimsies

Test 18
1) contained
2) disturbingly
3) compulsory
4) considerate
5) influence
6) tiredness
7) stretch
8) security
9) mandatory
10) annually

Test 19
1) renowned
2) transfusion
3) treatment
4) witnessed
5) resolved
6) syringe
7) donor
8) recipient
9) accomplished
10) devised

Test 20
1) perpetrated
2) Roundhead
3) acted
4) confiscated
5) villainous
6) knack
7) befriended
8) accomplices
9) stomach
10) stuffed
11) apprehended
12) Inexplicably
13) violent
14) granted
15) speculated
16) revenue
17) theories
18) embarrass
19) exhumed
20) faked

Test 21
1) epicentre
2) attributed
3) neighbourhood
4) tumbled
5) considerable
6) activity
7) inhabitants
8) ferocity
9) fault
10) underpin

Test 22
1) bestowed
2) conspicuous
3) distinction
4) appropriate
5) founding
6) Sovereign
7) Recipients
8) medallion
9) motto
10) politicians

Test 23
1) haunt
2) whitewashed
3) beaming
4) may
5) sunbeams
6) woody
7) trunks
8) shaded
9) cast
10) darkness
11) encountered
12) disbeliever
13) foray
14) galloped
15) turned
16) clap
17) jockey
18) overtaken
19) punch
20) bolted

Test 24
1) harrowing
2) accumulated
3) avalanche
4) debris
5) engulfing

Answers

6) nestling
7) shrouded
8) frantic
9) instability
10) criticised

Test 25
1) misconception
2) affordable
3) conveyance
4) assembly
5) repetitive
6) eager
7) adequately
8) committed
9) democratic
10) injustice

Test 26
1) portrayed
2) plaques
3) resembles
4) popular
5) sharply
6) superseded
7) constitutes
8) counterparts
9) respectively
10) suffix
11) gradually
12) identical
13) increased
14) evolved
15) revolutionary
16) proportions
17) tension
18) construction
19) obviated
20) debatable

Test 27
1) persuasions
2) movement
3) scream
4) writhing
5) grievous
6) gauged
7) folly
8) companion
9) knelt
10) breath

Test 28
1) emigrated
2) stylish
3) complexion
4) manufacture
5) pungent
6) accomplishment
7) concept
8) donning
9) faltered
10) perceived

Test 29
1) gentleman
2) able
3) bade
4) grave
5) fidgety
6) giggles
7) Swings
8) tilts
9) child
10) rude
11) cloth
12) matters
13) fret
14) tumbling
15) disgrace
16) Fairly
17) terrible
18) snapped
19) bare
20) dinner

Test 30
1) rural
2) diminutive
3) formal
4) contracted
5) stability
6) considerable
7) demonstrations
8) landslide
9) dignitaries
10) mourning

Test 31
1) shelter
2) rapidity
3) twilight
4) huddling
5) miseries
6) altitude
7) Suffice
8) exposure
9) vain
10) carcases

Test 32
1) ordinary
2) command
3) ranks
4) suffered
5) bouts

Answers

6) contemplated
7) frigate
8) set
9) island
10) settled
11) reserve
12) desperate
13) peacetime
14) recalled
15) declared
16) wounded
17) appointed
18) command
19) mortally
20) interred

Test 33
1) breeze
2) parched
3) wilt
4) circumstances
5) resolutions
6) fretful
7) forlorn
8) discomforts
9) languid
10) gazing

Test 34
1) airfield
2) determined
3) fund
4) cropped
5) aviators
6) gained
7) altitude
8) contended
9) circumnavigate
10) leg

Test 35
1) graced
2) estimated
3) surviving
4) ubiquitous
5) mounted
6) former
7) overseas
8) erected
9) uniform
10) adhesive
11) familiar
12) mainland
13) installed
14) capital
15) cylindrical
16) supermarkets
17) unique
18) skeleton
19) bunch
20) empty

Test 36
1) clutched
2) haul
3) scarce
4) bewilderment
5) struck
6) throb
7) giddy
8) tugged
9) violently
10) clambering

Test 37
1) building
2) spring
3) labour
4) light
5) crooked
6) twig
7) tuft
8) rainy
9) speak
10) together

Test 38
1) typhus
2) contracting
3) occupation
4) permit
5) nominated
6) creating
7) codename
8) auspices
9) safety
10) enormous
11) smuggle
12) ingenious
13) concealed
14) tolerated
15) pretext
16) solidarity
17) tortured
18) accomplices
19) execution
20) honours

Test 39
1) attributed
2) ascertain
3) substituted
4) overcame
5) density
6) preserved
7) disciplines
8) Modern
9) criminal
10) rational

Answers

11) confessions
12) used
13) conviction
14) found
15) shoot
16) identify
17) advocated
18) thumb
19) authenticity
20) pioneered

Test 40

1) contracted
2) communicate
3) developed
4) vocabulary
5) directed
6) impaired
7) frustrated
8) breakthrough
9) activist
10) advocate

PROGRESS CHARTS

Test	Mark	%
1		
2		
3		
4		
5		
6		
7		
8		
9		
10		
11		
12		
13		
14		
15		
16		
17		
18		
19		
20		

Test	Mark	%
21		
22		
23		
24		
25		
26		
27		
28		
29		
30		
31		
32		
33		
34		
35		
36		
37		
38		
38		
40		

Overall Percentage | %

CERTIFICATE OF

ACHIEVEMENT

This certifies

____

has successfully completed

11+ Verbal Activity

Year 5–7

TESTBOOK **7**

Overall percentage score achieved [   ] %

Comment ____________________________________

____

Signed ____________________________________

(teacher/parent/guardian)

Date ____________________________________